Private-Airplane Passenger Safety:

What You Need To Know

John O. Graybill

**FAA Designated Master Pilot, Commercial Pilot,
Certified Flight Instructor (CFI), Instrument Pilot**

Hand-Eye-Man Entertainment, LLC
6436 Del Paso Avenue
San Diego, CA 92120

Copyright © 2018 by John O. Graybill.
Photo on page 68 © John O. Graybill.
Photo on page 12 © Steve Homewood.
Photos on pages 16, 22, 94, 96, 112, 142, 155, 162, 178 © Chad Thompson
   Photography.
Photos on pages 8, 26, 28, 30, 35, 36, 54, 58, 74, 104, 106, 108, 116, 120, 124,
   128, 132, 136, 140, 148, 151, 158, 166, 170, 174, 182, 190, 194, 200 licensed
   from iStock.
Photos on pages 38, 44, 48, 60, 64, 84, 88, 98, 144, 186 licensed from
   Dreamstime.
Author photo on page 204 © Mark Ross Photography.

Book design by Monkey C Media, monkeyCmedia.com

Disclaimer: The material in this book is for informational purposes only
and is intended to supplement, not replace, private-airplane passenger
decision making. Like any activity involving speed, complex equipment,
multipart configurations, and environmental factors, being a passenger in
a private airplane always poses some inherent risk. In fact, using a private
airplane for travel may pose an increased risk over use of commercial
airlines, and therefore passengers assume full responsibility for their own
safety while traveling in a private airplane. The author and publisher
advise that the information contained in this book is, for the most part,
opinion based on experience. If you have any questions or concerns about
the contents of this book, please investigate other sources to your own
satisfaction in order to assure yourself that flying, or not flying, in a private
airplane is in your own best interest.

Printed in the United States
First Edition

ISBNs: 978-0-9997076-3-0 (hardcover),
            978-0-9997076-0-9 (trade paperback),
            978-0-9997076-1-6 (eBook),
            978-0-9997076-2-3 (ePub)

Library of Congress Control Number: 2017911781

This book is dedicated to the millions of private-airplane passengers, to their families, and to the pilots of those airplanes. May you always have enjoyable, incident-free, and safe flights in private airplanes.

Contents

Forward

John O. Graybill has been a friend since our days in high school when we both learned to fly as teenagers. Although our aviation careers are quite different, we have always remained connected through our common love of aviation.

As a captain for United Airlines, I have always been concerned about the comfort and safety of my passengers. However, private-airplane passengers, in many cases, may not enjoy the same level of concern by their pilots nor be able to evaluate any aspect of the performance of their pilots.

This book takes a big step forward by providing private-airplane passengers with a specific set of observations of pilot behavior that are useful in making decisions about the pilot in command of their flights in private airplanes.

Mr. Graybill has been an active aviator for some fifty years, flying private airplanes while carrying nonpilot passengers. He has always been sensitive to helping people who are reluctant to fly in private airplanes, and he has always been sensitive to his passengers' concerns, fears, and any problems they may have experienced during their flight with him as pilot.

After reading this book, people who fly as passengers in private airplanes will feel much more comfortable, confident, and better able to understand the safe practices of their private-airplane pilots.

—Dale Salem, United Airlines B747 Captain (ret.)

Private-Airplane Passenger Safety: How to Survive Being a Private-Airplane Passenger

The purpose of this guide is to help nonpilot passengers who fly in private airplanes, or who are considering flying as a passenger in a private airplane, to understand whether or not the intended flight will be as safe as it can be before takeoff. Many private-airplane passengers have no idea whether or not their pilot is about to conduct a safe flight or a very risky one. Most private-airplane accidents are the result of one or more bad actions taken by the pilot. This guide will alert you to pilot actions, behaviors, and attitudes that could lead to a crash, personal injury, or worse.

1

Airplane Safety

*Flying as a passenger in
private airplanes is, in general, safe.*

Moreover, traveling by private airplane can be a wonderful and enjoyable experience that provides a convenient means of personal transportation. However, it is important to remember that when flying in a private airplane, your safety is in the hands of the pilot who is in command of your flight. The moment you board a private airplane, you relinquish all control of the flight to the pilot. At that moment, your survival depends on the pilot because he or she is not only responsible for providing a safe flight but also for ensuring that the airplane is mechanically airworthy and that the weather you encounter will not be too much for the airplane and flight crew to handle safely.

The paragraphs within this guide describe practices, behaviors, and attitudes that private-airplane passengers may observe on the part of their pilot and are marked as follows:

Red Flag: A blatantly bad practice that significantly increases the chance of having a serious accident or crash that results in grave injuries or death.

 Yellow Flag: Generally a bad practice that might contribute to an accident or unpleasant and/or frightening experience. A yellow flag practice by itself may not necessarily be unsafe but may add to the risk of the flight.

If you are a passenger on a flight and observe a single red flag or three or more yellow flags, you would be wise to not proceed with the flight.

Most of the observations described below can be observed before the flight; others can only be observed during the flight, in which case all you can do is make a mental note for your consideration on future flights. Don't be troubled if you are unable to see all of the pilot behaviors described here. The idea is to reconsider your plans to be a private-airplane passenger if you observe one red or three yellow observations, even if you are unable to observe the majority of behaviors described here.

Although less likely to be observed on private jet airplanes and/or commercial charter operations than on single-engine private airplanes, for the most part, these red-flag and yellow-flag observations are just as applicable.

Alternatively, if after careful observation you conclude that the behaviors, actions, and attitudes of your pilot do not merit any red flags or yellow flags, you can be confident that your flight will most likely be comfortable, safe, and generally comparable to riding as a passenger in an automobile.

Airplane
Condition

2

UNITED STATES OF AMERICA
DEPARTMENT OF TRANSPORTATION—FEDERAL AVIATION ADMINISTRATION

STANDARD AIRWORTHINESS CERTIFICATE

1 NATIONALITY AND REGISTRATION MARKS	2 MANUFACTURER AND MODEL		3 AIRCRAFT SERIAL NUMBER	4 CATEGORY
N60458	Cessna Aircraft Company	T182T	T18208574	Normal

5 AUTHORITY AND BASIS FOR ISSUANCE

This airworthiness certificate is issued pursuant to the Federal Aviation Act of 1958 and certifies that, as of the date of issuance, the aircraft to which issued has been inspected and found to conform to the type certificate therefor, to be in condition for safe operation, and has been shown to meet the requirements of the applicable comprehensive and detailed airworthiness code as provided by Annex 8 to the Convention on International Civil Aviation, except as noted herein. Exceptions:

NONE

6. TERMS AND CONDITIONS

Unless sooner surrendered, suspended, revoked, or a termination date is otherwise established by the Administrator, this airworthiness certificate is effective as long as the maintenance, preventative maintenance, and alterations are performed in accordance with Parts 21, 43, and 91 of the Federal Aviation Regulations, as appropriate, and the aircraft is registered in the United States.

DATE OF ISSUANCE	FAA REPRESENTATIVE	DESIGNATION NUMBER
06/26/2006	Benjamin Shufelt	ODARF100129CE

Any alteration, reproduction, or misuse of this certificate may be punishable by a fine not exceeding $1,000, or imprisonment not exceeding 3 years, or both. THIS CERTIFICATE MUST BE DISPLAYED IN THE AIRCRAFT IN ACCORDANCE WITH APPLICABLE FEDERAL AVIATION REGULATIONS.

FAA Form 8100-2 (8-82)

∗ U.S. G.P.O.:2003 668-291

You are unable to see the Federal Aviation Administration (FAA) airworthiness certificate for the airplane in which you will be a passenger.

FAA regulations require that the airworthiness certificate be posted within the airplane cabin in plain sight.

In smaller airplanes, the airworthiness certificate is often posted in a clear plastic envelope on the sidewall of the cabin near the floor near the left pilot seat. If the pilot cannot show you where the airworthiness certificate is posted inside the cabin, you should not agree to be a passenger in the airplane.

There is no acceptable excuse for flying an airplane that does not have a posted airworthiness certificate.

Lack of an airworthiness certificate could indicate that the airplane's certificate was revoked by the FAA because the airplane no longer meets its approved design and is therefore not airworthy.

Lack of a certificate also raises questions about the airplane's

- structural integrity;
- correctness of airplane system functions;
- history of required airplane inspections; and
- ownership custody, including the possibility that the airplane is stolen.

Before the flight, you notice amateur-looking repairs or modifications on the airplane.

FAA regulations require that most mechanical repairs or modifications to an airplane be done by FAA-certified mechanics and inspectors. Any sign of nonstandard repairs or modifications should cause you to think yellow flag. Repairs involving "temporary" fixes with duct tape, safety wire, oversized or nonstandard screws or fasteners, or common hardware-store nuts and bolts should be viewed with suspicion and make you think yellow flag.

Before the flight, you notice the word "EXPERIMENTAL" prominently displayed on either the inside or outside of the airplane.

In most cases this means that the airplane was built by a private individual and that its construction does not fully comply with the regulations governing the production of factory-built FAA-certified airplanes. In all cases experimental airplanes do not comply with the FAA regulations governing the manufacture of certified factory-built airplanes. Experimental airplanes have a slightly higher fatality rate as compared to certified factory-built airplanes. So think yellow flag if the airplane to be used is designated as experimental.

While landing the airplane at your planned destination, your pilot makes a rough landing, causing the wingtip or tail of the airplane to strike the ground.

Your pilot examines the damage and announces that the damage is inconsequential and that it is safe to fly the airplane back to the departure airport the next day. Unless your pilot is an FAA-certified aircraft mechanic, he or she is not qualified to make that call, and any damage to the airplane should be inspected by someone who is. To forego a review of the damage by a certified mechanic should definitely make you think yellow flag.

Pilot Condition

3

Your pilot appears to have consumed alcohol sometime within eight hours before the planned departure time.

It is a violation of FAA regulations—and it's dangerous—for anyone to fly an airplane anytime within eight hours of consuming any amount of alcohol. Even a little alcohol consumed by a pilot can be a big problem once an airplane gains altitude. The thinner air at higher altitudes can increase the intoxicating effects of alcohol. Heavy binge drinking the night before a flight can still be a problem, even if the required eight hours has expired. You should not agree to be a passenger in a private airplane if you believe that the pilot might be intoxicated—even just a little—from alcohol consumption or drug use.

Your pilot mentions that he or she is going through some kind of emotional turmoil, such as divorce, recent death of a loved one, or some other personal crisis.

There have been fatal airplane accidents that were directly related to the pilot's personal problems. So think yellow flag if your pilot is going through a personal crisis.

Operations Checklist

Parking Brake	
Fuel Flow	Set
Battery Switch	Cutoff
Hydraulic Pump ON	On
Landing Gear	On
Flaps	Check
Spoiler	Up
Fuel Amount	Retracted
De-Ice	Check
Passenger Sign	Off
Check Weather	Off
	Flight Services
Transponder	
Anti Collision Ligths	Standby
	On
...ine Start Swiches	
...mp Switche	Check
...arter Switch	On
	On
...e	On
	Check
...ts	On
...nts	Check
	Set Departure
	Off
	On

You notice that your pilot seems to exercise his or her pilot duties by rote memory and does not use written checklists.

Airplanes are complex machines consisting of numerous interrelated subsystems. In order for them to function successfully, many switches, levers, and controls must be selected, operated, and positioned in accordance with the flight situation—preflight inspection, engine starting, taxi to the takeoff runway, run-up of the engine(s), takeoff, climb, cruise, descent, approach, landing, taxi to parking, and engine(s) shutdown. There have been many airplane accidents that resulted from a pilot's failure to select some critical item. So think yellow flag if it appears that your pilot does not use written checklists to guide him or her in the step-by-step execution of cockpit duties.

A very important item on the pre-takeoff checklist is the "control check." This is achieved when the pilot moves all of the controls in the cockpit while looking to verify correct movement of the ailerons and flaps on the wings and tail controls by direct observation or by looking at indicators in the cockpit. You should definitely think yellow flag if you notice that your pilot takes off without checking the movement of the controls.

Night Flying

4

Before a flight at night, you learn that your pilot has not flown at night within the preceding ninety days.

It is a violation of FAA regulations for anyone to fly an airplane with passengers at night if they have not flown at night during the preceding ninety days. It is unwise to fly at night if the pilot has not flown at night for many months or years. This is referred to as "night currency," and there have been fatal crashes related to a pilot's lack of recent night-flying experience. If you believe that flying at night is likely, think red flag if there are no flashlights on board the airplane or if you believe that your pilot has not flown at night for many months or years.

5

Flying in Clouds

Before a flight you believe is likely to enter clouds, you learn that your pilot does not have an instrument rating or has not flown in cloudy conditions for many months or years.

A very large percentage of fatal airplane accidents involve pilots who attempted to fly into clouds or fog with no instrument rating and/or no, or little, experience and/or training in cloud flying. If your pilot does not appear to be completely qualified to fly in clouds (i.e., in "instrument conditions"), you will be putting your life in real jeopardy if you elect to make the flight into clouds as his or her passenger. "Completely qualified" means that your pilot has an instrument rating and has met the recent experience requirements as defined by the FAA regulations.

In order to qualify for an instrument rating, a pilot must have taken a rigorous written examination and a comprehensive flight test administered by a federally designated pilot examiner. The situation is especially risky if your flight occurs in the clouds at night.

Think red flag if your pilot is not able to easily and clearly tell you about his or her journey to obtain the instrument rating and his or her recent experience flying in clouds solely by reference to instruments. Otherwise, you should strongly reconsider your decision to be a passenger on the flight.

Student Pilot

6

Your pilot mentions that he or she has been taking a lot of flying lessons recently and is very close to obtaining the private pilot certificate.

Although a pilot can be certified by the FAA as a student pilot with certain limited flight privileges, it would be a violation of FAA regulations for a student pilot to carry passengers in his or her airplane. If the pilot possesses a student pilot certificate, he or she is authorized to fly only when he or she is the sole occupant of the airplane— and then only when a certified flight instructor (CFI) has approved and is supervising the flight from the ground. It would be unwise to fly as a passenger when the pilot possesses only a student pilot certificate. So think red flag if you believe that your pilot is not authorized to carry passengers, and do not get in the airplane.

7

Pilot Experience

You get the impression that your pilot has not flown in many months or years.

FAA regulations require every pilot to have flown a certain amount during the preceding ninety days. Moreover, every pilot is required to receive at least one hour of flight instruction and one hour of ground instruction from an FAA CFI once every twenty-four months.

It is a very bad practice, and illegal, for a pilot to fly an airplane if he or she has not flown for a long period of time. Think yellow flag if your pilot gives the impression that he or she has not flown for a while and might be "a little rusty."

Your pilot mentions that he or she is a new pilot with fewer than five hundred hours of total flight time.

You should think yellow flag if your pilot is relatively new to aviation and has accumulated fewer than five hundred hours of total flight time. Although very new pilots may be safer due to an abundance of caution driven by their new status as airplane pilots, there is an unverified theory that at the range of four hundred to six hundred flight hours, some pilots may become overconfident, which could lead to trouble.

Some studies suggest that the riskiest range of flight hours is from 50 to 350 hours of total flight time. In general, the fewer flight hours your pilot has accumulated, the higher the risk of an accident. It is not uncommon for new pilots to arrange for a more experienced "mentor-pilot" to accompany him or her on longer flights to unfamiliar airports.

Weight Distribution

Your pilot appears unconcerned about where in the airplane people and baggage are loaded.

Under some circumstances, airplanes that have been loaded improperly or have been severely overloaded can become uncontrollable, which can lead to a crash. Most private airplanes have placards posted in or near the baggage compartments that list the maximum allowed weight of the compartment contents. Your pilot should be concerned about where people and objects are located in the airplane when it is flying. You should be concerned if you believe that the airplane might be improperly loaded or significantly overloaded. For example, if all of the big people and too much heavy baggage is stowed in the back and only the small pilot is in the front, this might not be safe for some airplanes. So feel comforted if your pilot seems concerned about weight distribution within the airplane.

Frosty Wings

When you and the other passengers arrive at the airport early on a very cold morning, you notice that your pilot seems unconcerned about the frost (or ice) covering the wings of the airplane.

There have been fatal accidents resulting from pilots who have attempted to take off with frost (or ice) on an airplane's wings. For a variety of technical aerodynamic reasons, airplanes have great difficulty getting airborne when the wings are covered with frost. Even though frost often appears benign, attempting to take off with frost (or ice) on the wings will most certainly result in a horrible crash. You should definitely be thinking red flag if your pilot indicates that he or she is going to attempt to take off with frost on the wings of the airplane.

Before attempting a takeoff, your pilot should be absolutely certain that every bit of frost and/or ice is removed from the wings. There are several options for clearing the wings, including waiting until it warms up enough to melt the frost or ice into water droplets, moving the airplane into a heated hangar, having the airplane sprayed with deicing fluid, or physically removing the frost and ice with gloved hands and/or rags. This is definitely a red-flag event, and you should not agree to be a passenger if the airplane's wings are contaminated with frost and/or ice.

10

Pilot Arrival

On the day of departure, your pilot has arranged for you and the other passengers to arrive at the airplane at approximately the same time that he or she arrives.

This is a bad practice because interacting with passengers while the pilot is preparing for the flight can be very distracting to the pilot, which can lead to him or her overlooking something that is important to the safety of the flight. Ideally your pilot should arrive at least one hour before your arrival at the departure airport. This should give the pilot time to prepare for the flight. This is less critical if you are flying on a private jet or if you are flying on a properly licensed and certified commercial charter operation that includes multiple pilots and one or more flight attendants who are able to assist with your luggage and with getting you seated. Similarly, this is less critical if your private jet is flying to the departure airport to pick you up. However, even when being picked up, you should think yellow flag if you sense that your pilot seems rushed to get the airplane ready for the next leg of the trip with you as passenger.

If your flight is a return flight where you, the other passengers, and the pilot arrive back at the airport together, you would be wise to resist the temptation to "help" the pilot load the airplane with luggage and with the other things required to get the airplane ready for the return flight. Unless you have been briefed, and unless you are familiar with the specific tasks required to get the airplane ready for the return flight, you run the risk that your helping gestures will distract the pilot and contribute to him or her missing some important "make-ready" tasks.

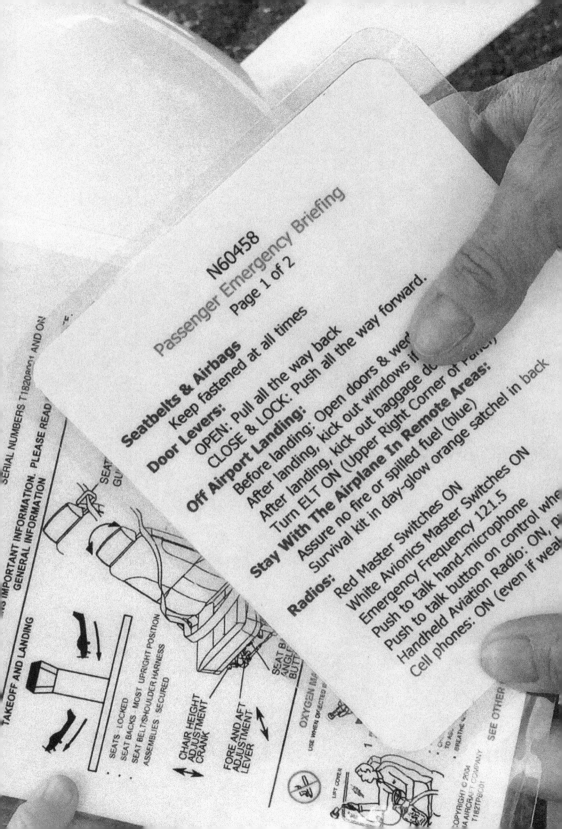

N60458
Passenger Emergency Briefing
Page 1 of 2

Seatbelts & Airbags
Keep fastened at all times

Door Levers:
OPEN: Pull all the way back
CLOSE & LOCK: Push all the way forward.

Off Airport Landing:
Before landing: Open doors & we
After landing, kick out baggage do
After landing, kick out windows if
Turn ELT ON (Upper Right Corner of Panel)

Stay With The Airplane In Remote Areas:
Assure no fire or spilled fuel (blue)
Survival kit in day-glow orange satchel in back

Radios:
Red Master Switches ON
White Avionics Master Switches ON
Emergency Frequency 121.5
Push to talk hand-microphone
Push to talk button on control whe
Handheld Aviation Radio: ON, p
Cell phones: ON (even if wea

SERIAL NUMBERS T1820P001 AND ON

IMPORTANT INFORMATION. PLEASE READ
GENERAL INFORMATION

TAKEOFF AND LANDING

SEATS - LOCKED
SEAT BACKS - MOST UPRIGHT POSITION
SEAT BELT/SHOULDER HARNESS
ASSEMBLIES SECURED

CHAIR HEIGHT
ADJUSTMENT
CRANK

FORE AND AFT
ADJUSTMENT
LEVER

SEAT
GU

SEAT B
ANGLE
BUTT

OXYGEN M

USE WHEN DIRECTED BY

LIFT COVER

SEE OTHER

COPYRIGHT © 20
A AIRCRAFT COMPANY
T182TP8C01

Your pilot fails to provide a preflight passenger briefing.

It is bad practice to not provide a passenger briefing before a flight. Well-prepared pilots will provide their passengers with passenger briefing checklists on laminated cards. Moreover, FAA regulations require that the pilot in command ensures that all passengers are briefed before a flight on such things as:

During the flight

- How to buckle and unbuckle the seat belts and shoulder harnesses.

- How to open the doors and emergency exits.

- How to operate any handheld radios stored in the airplane cabin.

- When passengers should refrain from talking during the flight.

- How to operate the intercom headsets and microphones.

- How to operate the fire extinguisher.

After an "off-airport landing" (i.e., after a "crash landing")

- The need for adequate clothing.

- The use of cell phones.

- The function and operation of the emergency locator transmitter.

- The decision to stay with the plane versus attempting to walk out.

- The location of first-aid and survival gear.

11

Preflight Rush

Your pilot appears to be rushed, preoccupied, and impatient as he or she prepares for the flight.

Your pilot should not appear to be rushing or impatient to get fuel, load baggage, check weather forecasts, file a flight plan, arrange for lodging, and get or turn in a rental car, all with the hope of beating approaching foul weather or impending darkness. Many private-airplane accidents have been related to the pilot overlooking a safety item because he or she was rushing to beat some perceived deadline. Think yellow flag if your pilot appears to be impatient and rushing to get ready for the flight.

12

Preflight Inspection

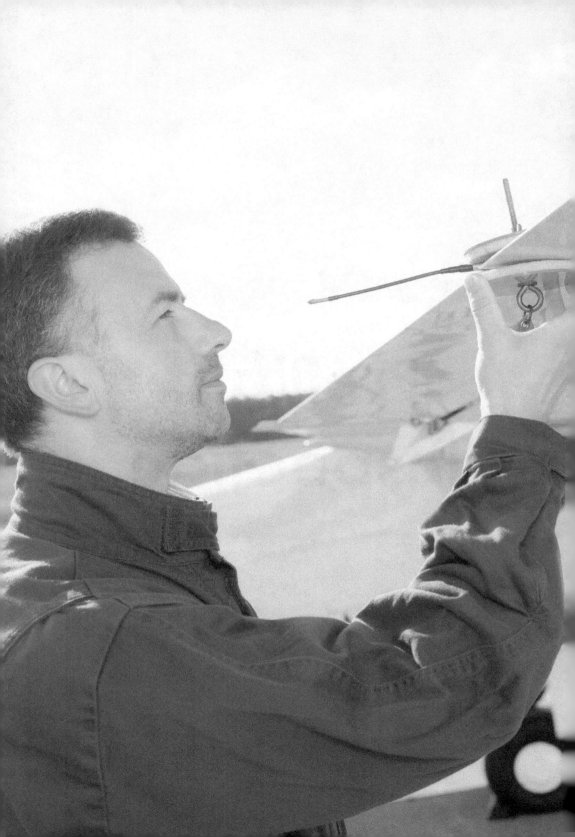

Your pilot fails to perform a preflight walk-around inspection of the airplane just before the flight.

Fatal crashes have occurred when the pilot did not notice damage to the airplane because he or she failed to conduct a thorough preflight inspection of the airplane.

The preflight inspection is the responsibility of the pilot who is in command of the airplane. There are some items on some airplanes that can lead to a crash if they are not attended to during the preflight inspection. For example, metal control locks are often placed on the wings or on the controls within the airplane cabin in order to prevent damage to the wing and tail controls from gusty winds when the airplane is parked. Control locks hold the wing and tail controls fast so that they are not moved by the wind when parked. Failure to remove a control lock before a flight can result in a catastrophic crash.

Normally, control locks placed on the outside of the airplane have bright-red flags attached with printed words that say "Remove Before Flight." Think yellow flag if your pilot seems uninterested in conducting a thorough pre-flight inspection.

Fuel Levels

Your pilot elects to proceed with the flight with a minimum load of fuel.

Decisions regarding how much fuel to put in the airplane can be complex and may be related to the total weight of the fuel, baggage, people, and/or anticipated headwinds or tailwinds. Think yellow flag if your pilot appears to be primarily motivated by the cost of the fuel rather than the loading of the correct number of gallons to ensure that the flight can be made safely with plenty of fuel left over as a reserve. In most circumstances, your pilot should plan to arrive at your destination with no less than one hour of fuel still in the airplane fuel tanks. That is to say, your "fuel reserve" should be no less than one hour.

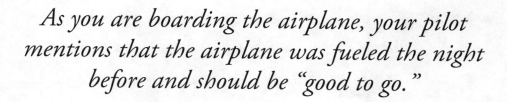

As you are boarding the airplane, your pilot mentions that the airplane was fueled the night before and should be "good to go."

It is a risky practice for a pilot to take off without physically verifying that a sufficient amount of fuel is actually in the airplane's fuel tanks. If the tanks are thought to be full, the pilot should remove the fuel tank cap, peer into the tank, and thereby confirm that the tanks are indeed full of fuel.

If it is thought that the fuel tanks are partially full, a clear plastic straw-like dipstick can be used to physically verify the quantity of fuel in each of the airplane's fuel tanks.

The same goes for verifying that there is a sufficient amount of oil in the engine. So if your pilot just assumes that the fuel and oil are "good to go" without physical verification, think yellow flag.

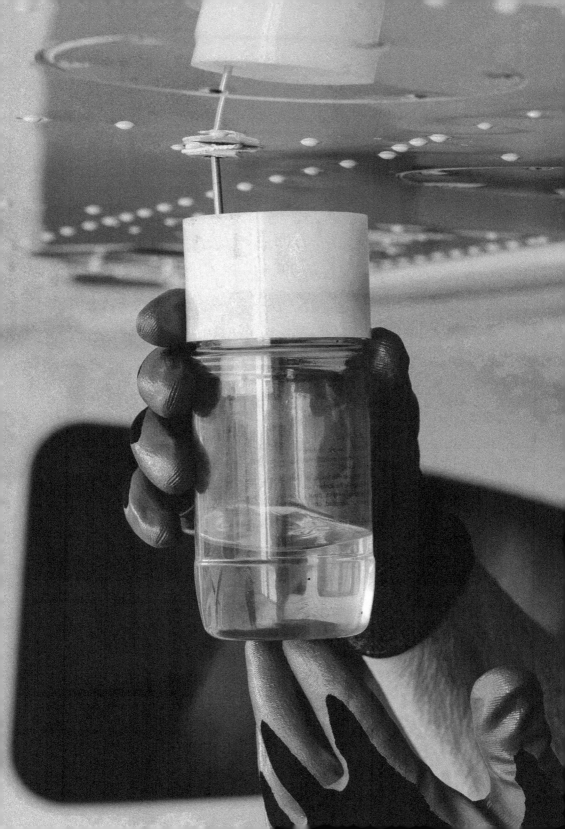

When your flight is the first flight of the day for the airplane, or the airplane has just been fueled, you notice that your pilot does not examine any fuel samples.

Airplane fuel (Avgas) contaminated with water or other substances has resulted in fatal crashes. There have been cases where condensation has formed overnight on the inside of partially filled fuel tanks and then has run down to the low points inside the fuel tanks only to be drawn into the engine, causing it to run rough or even fail.

Inspecting fuel by sampling involves use of a specially configured clear plastic sampling cup. Think yellow flag if you believe that your pilot is not sampling fuel from each of the tanks and from the engine in the airplane to examine for water or other contamination. Water is heavier than Avgas and will settle into the low points within the fuel tanks and related plumbing. Typically a drain sump is located at each of the low points of the fuel system. Some private airplanes have as many as thirteen drain sumps. When a sample is taken through one of the drain sumps, water is easily detected.

14

Weather Conditions

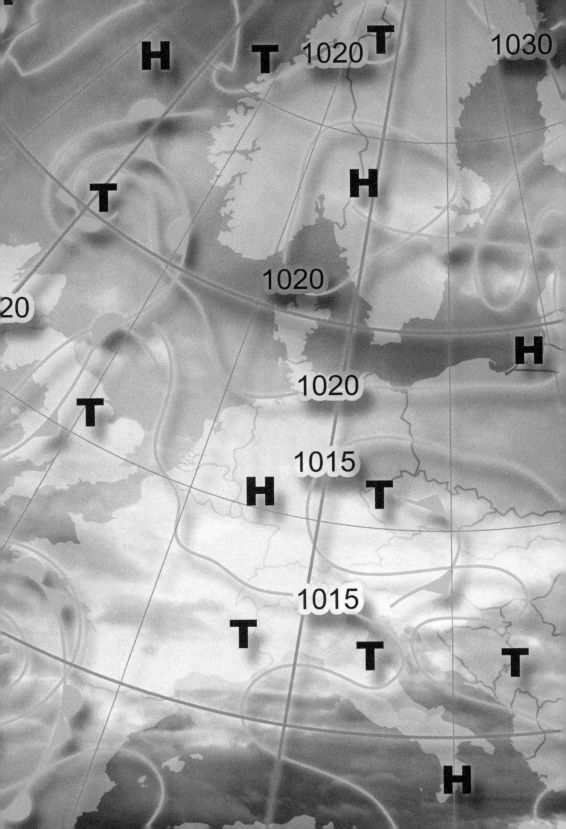

You get the impression that your pilot is not fully aware of the weather conditions along the intended route of flight.

Weak knowledge about the current and forecast weather conditions for the intended route of flight has been a factor in many fatal airplane crashes. There are countless ways for a pilot to obtain good information about the weather, including the Internet and government-provided flight-service sources. Your pilot should give the impression that he or she is in tune with the pertinent weather facts relevant to your intended route of flight. Otherwise, think yellow flag.

Your pilot appears to have a casual attitude about flying near thunderstorms.

Many airplane accidents have involved pilots flying too near, or in, thunderstorms. Some thunderstorms produce enough energy to dismember airplanes. Most thunderstorms should be circumvented by at least twenty-five miles. Your pilot should have a very serious attitude about thunderstorm avoidance. If your pilot appears to disrespect thunderstorms, think yellow flag.

While still on the ground before departure, your pilot mentions that your flight is probably going to encounter turbulence during the flight.

In the vast majority of cases, turbulence is only an uncomfortable annoyance and not a significant additional risk. The amount of turbulence that can be expected is forecast every few hours by the National Oceanic Atmospheric Administration (NOAA) and is available on the Internet. Turbulence forecasts come in four levels of intensity:

- *Light little "bumps"*

- *Moderate light-plus, but airplane remains in positive control*

- *Severe large bumps, airplane momentarily out of control*

- *Extreme violent bumps that cause damage to the airplane*

Although unpleasant for many people, light to moderate turbulence adds only an infinitesimal bit of risk to the flight. On the other hand, you probably will not be happy if your flight encounters severe or extreme turbulence. If your pilot suggests light or moderate turbulence should be expected, then this observation can be treated as a normal yellow flag observation. If severe or extreme turbulence is anticipated, you may want to raise a red flag, in which case your pilot may decide to delay the flight or plan for a different route where less turbulence is forecast. In any event, it is up to you to ask what level of turbulence intensity is forecast for the planned route of flight.

While still on the ground before departure, your pilot mentions that your flight is probably going to encounter strong headwinds during the flight, which means that the flight will take more time to complete than it would if there were no headwinds.

Headwinds also mean that more fuel will be consumed than would be if there were no headwinds. There have been private-airplane accidents because of strong headwinds that led to fuel exhaustion. If your pilot suggests that headwinds are likely, you might ask if he or she believes the fuel load is sufficient to make it to the destination in spite of the headwinds. If there is any question about whether or not the fuel load is sufficient to overcome the headwinds, you should think yellow flag.

15

Supplemental Oxygen

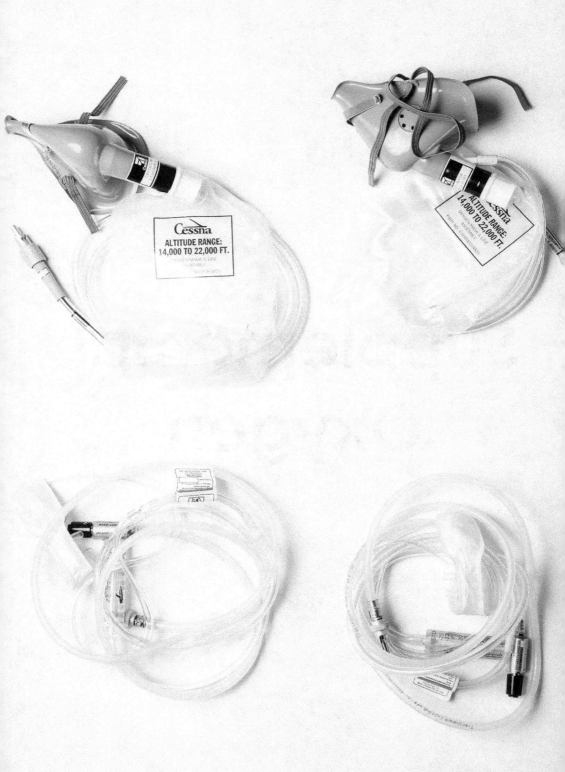

Before the flight, your pilot indicates that he or she plans part of the flight to be conducted in an unpressurized airplane at an altitude above fifteen thousand feet with little or no supplemental oxygen available to the pilot and passengers.

FAA regulations require the use of supplemental oxygen in unpressurized airplanes above fifteen thousand feet. Flying at such altitudes in unpressurized airplanes without oxygen is a bad idea. Lack of oxygen, known as hypoxia, could result in the incapacitation of the pilot. The use of supplemental oxygen is especially important if the intended flight at these higher altitudes is planned to take place at night because lack of oxygen impairs night vision well before other symptoms of hypoxia will be noticed. So if your pilot plans to fly at high altitudes at night without supplemental oxygen, think yellow flag.

Inspection Intervals

16

Before the flight, your pilot gives the impression that he or she does not strictly comply with all of the federally mandated inspection intervals for the airplane.

FAA regulations require many of the systems and parts of the airplane to be inspected and repaired or recalibrated, if necessary, at specified intervals. Although complying with these inspection and repair mandates can be annoying and expensive, failure to do so can be dangerous if a defect goes undetected. Indeed, the entire airplane and all of its systems must be thoroughly inspected annually. Think yellow flag if you suspect that your pilot, or the airplane's owner, is not ensuring that all required inspections and repairs have been undertaken— especially if you suspect that your pilot or the airplane's owner has allowed more than one year to lapse since the last annual inspection.

High-Altitude Takeoff

17

Your pilot exhibits a cavalier attitude about taking off from an airport that is located more than four thousand feet above sea level on a very hot day.

A pilot who attempts to fly a fully loaded airplane without a turbocharged engine from an airport that is more than four thousand feet above sea level on a very hot day may never leave the ground. If the airplane does become airborne during its takeoff run, it may simply skim just a few feet above the ground until it hits obstacles at the end of the runway. For a number of technical reasons, airplanes suffer diminished performance at high altitudes when the air is hot. In any event, think yellow flag when you suspect that your pilot is going to attempt to take off from a high-altitude airport on a hot day in a fully loaded airplane with you aboard.

The pilot's operating handbook for the airplane contains tables that show the amount of runway needed to get airborne for a given total airplane weight, wind velocity, runway condition, and temperature. Again, think yellow flag if you believe that your pilot has not referred to these tables for high-altitude airports on a hot day.

18

Icing Conditions

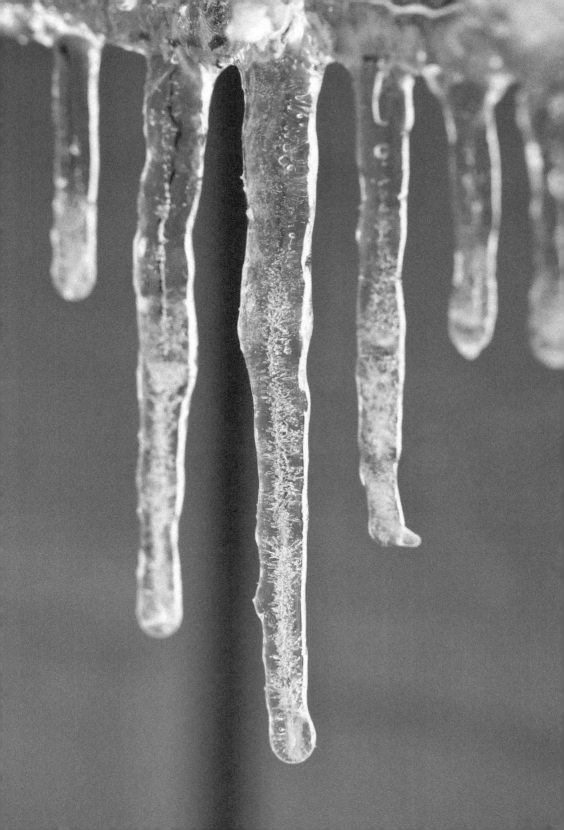

Your pilot casually mentions that there is a good chance of encountering icing conditions during your intended flight.

Flying in icing conditions—which almost always occurs while flying in clouds—without deicing equipment on the airplane can be very risky. When ice accumulates on an airplane's wings and tail, the airplane can become very difficult to control. Crashes have resulted from excessive ice accumulation on an airplane's wings and tail.

Icing can usually be avoided by flying around, above, or below clouds when the temperature outside of the airplane is at, or near, freezing. If your pilot seems overly willing to fly in icing conditions without deicing equipment, think yellow flag. Your pilot should be very concerned about avoiding icing conditions.

19

Buzzing

Your pilot offers to fly you and the other passengers over your house or over a stadium, beach, park, or other area that is full of people.

There have been tragic airplane crashes that involved pilots showing off to their passengers by flying low over their houses or over gatherings of people on the ground. Unless your pilot is a professional airshow stunt pilot or is otherwise well trained in low-level aerobatics, such flying can easily lead to sad and tragic airplane crashes that can kill the pilot and passengers as well as people on the ground. This type of flying is often referred to as "buzzing" and should be avoided.

Pilot Judgment

20

Your pilot has made a decision to not proceed or to land at an alternate airport due to adverse weather, and you are tempted to try to coax him or her to proceed with the original flight anyway.

There have been fatal airplane accidents that were related to passengers cajoling the pilot to make a flight he or she was reluctant to make. Doing this is not wise and has a good chance of leading the flight to an unhappy and tragic conclusion. Think yellow flag if you find yourself trying to convince the pilot to make a flight that he or she feels would be unsafe or risky.

21

Airplane Propellers

You notice that your pilot appears to show no fear or respect of the propeller(s) on the airplane.

Although propeller accidents are rare, they have occurred, and they are always very ugly. You should treat every propeller like a loaded gun. There have been numerous terrible accidents involving airplane passengers being struck by turning propellers.

If the airplane uses an ignition key, your pilot should not leave the airplane unattended with the ignition key in the ignition switch. Your pilot should encourage his or her passengers to not touch the propeller and to remain clear of its arc. Think yellow flag if your pilot does not appear to respect the airplane's propellers.

When starting the airplane engine(s),
you notice that the pilot's window is
closed and that he or she starts the engine
without first shouting "clear."

Even if it appears that no one is near the propeller(s), it is not a good practice to start the airplane engine(s) without first shouting this warning: "clear" or "clear prop." Moreover, the pilot should ensure that the wheel brakes are locked before starting the engine(s). You should think yellow flag if your pilot starts the engine(s) without shouting "clear" or "clear prop" first, or if you sense that the wheel brakes are not locked because you notice that the airplane moves forward when the engine(s) starts.

Your pilot informs you that in order to save time, he or she will keep the engine(s) running while another passenger boards the airplane at an intermediate stop.

In almost all circumstances, this is a really bad idea because of the risk that the boarding passenger will walk into the turning propeller. This has happened and is almost always fatal. Boarding a passenger might be done safely if he or she is a highly experienced aviator and is very familiar with your pilot, the airplane, and the airport environment. In order to save time, it can be very tempting to condone the boarding of a passenger when the propeller is turning, but in most cases, doing so should make you think red flag.

22

Pilot Concentration

You observe that your pilot talks to his or her passengers a lot while flying near very busy airspace near large commercial airports.

Typically for longer trips, the first and last parts of private-airplane flights take place in active airspace near larger airports. If your pilot has not encouraged you to minimize talking while flying in these areas, or during the takeoff or landing, you would be wise to do so on your own accord. During these parts of the flight, your pilot can get very busy and might miss some critical flight-safety items if the pilot and passengers are engaged in heavy conversation. Many airlines actually prohibit their pilots from engaging in unnecessary talking during these critical parts of the flight. So think yellow flag if you hear a lot of talking from your pilot during these times.

Your pilot notifies you that during your flight, he or she will do some formation flying with a fellow pilot friend in another airplane so as to take photographs of the two airplanes in midair.

Unless the participating pilots have had special training in formation flying, this could turn out to be a bad idea. Formation flying is not easy and can lead to awful outcomes if done improperly. Think yellow flag if your pilot says that he or she wants to take you on a formation flight with another airplane.

23

Open-Toed Shoes

You notice that your pilot is wearing open-toed shoes when walking near the airplane when it is parked and secured by ropes or chains to the ground. Or the pilot does not encourage you to wear closed-toed shoes.

Because most airplanes can be upset and damaged by a gust of wind or a blast of air from a helicopter that is landing or taking off, most airports provide hard points that are buried in the ground or asphalt so that ropes or chains can be attached to them. These hard points are usually made of steel and may be dangerously jagged and sharp. Consequently, open-toed footwear can lead to bloody toes and are not recommended when walking on airport property. So think yellow flag if your pilot seems unconcerned about wearing open-toed shoes around airport tie-down hard points.

24

Airplane Altitude

You notice that when your pilot is talking on the airplane radio, he or she does not mention the airplane altitude when maneuvering for landing or taking off from an airport that does not have an FAA control tower.

Because most airports do not have an FAA control tower, pilots use the airplane radio to "self-report" their position and altitude to any other airplanes in the area. This procedure minimizes the possibility of a midair conflict with other airplanes. Because airplanes cannot collide unless they are both at the exact same altitude, it is very important that your pilot include the altitude of the airplane in every one of the position reports he or she broadcasts over the airplane radio when maneuvering near an airport that does not have an FAA control tower. This will allow any other airplanes that are at or near your altitude to take evasive action to prevent a midair collision. Your pilot's failure to include altitude in each of his or her position reports should make you think yellow flag.

25

Unattended Airplane

Your pilot shows no concern about leaving the airplane not tied down or secured while he or she and all of the passengers are away from the airport.

M ost private airplanes are relatively light and can be upset or otherwise damaged by gusty winds, propeller blasts from other nearby airplanes, or a helicopter's rotor blast. Your pilot's failure to properly secure the airplane while it is unattended may reflect an attitude that is not generally conducive to safe practices. Think yellow flag if your pilot exhibits a willingness to leave the airplane unattended and unsecured to the ground for long periods of time.

Fog

26

When you arrive at the airport, you notice that everything is covered in dense fog.

Although it may be legal for a pilot to take off when the visibility and ceiling are zero or near zero, doing so definitely increases the risk of an accident. Any problems encountered during takeoff after lifting off into dense fog will be much more difficult to handle as compared to flying under normal ceilings and visibilities. Plans to fly in "zero/zero" ceiling and visibility conditions should make you think yellow flag.

27

Destination Changes

Midflight to a planned destination, your pilot announces that he or she plans to change the destination.

This should raise a yellow flag—especially if the pilot has never landed at the new, unplanned destination. This sudden change in plans could mean that the pilot has not taken the time to properly plan for flying over the course to the new destination and has not determined whether or not there are intervening mountains on the way to the new destination or that the airport at the new destination is open and available for use.

28

Radar Services

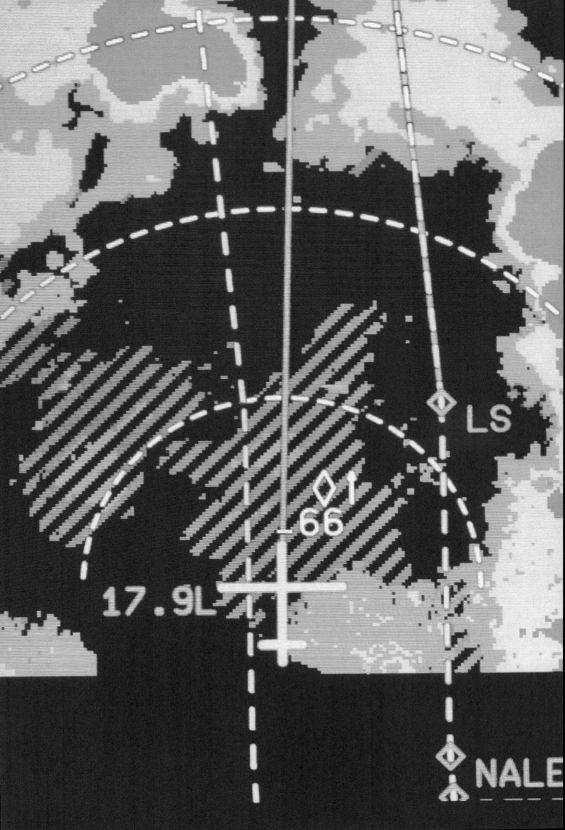

You notice that your pilot does not appear to be using the radar flight-following services that are provided by the FAA.

If your pilot uses radar flight-following services, he or she will receive spoken communications by means of the onboard aircraft radio from a radar controller on the ground anytime your flight gets too close to other airplanes. There is no charge for these services; without them it can be very difficult to see other airplanes that might pose a midair collision threat. Failure to use the FAA-provided radar flight-following services should make you think yellow flag.

29

Flight Plans

Form Approved: OMB No. 2120-0026
Exp. 05/31/2017

FLIGHT PLAN

U.S. DEPARTMENT OF TRANSPORTATION
FEDERAL AVIATION ADMINISTRATION

(FAA USE ONLY)	☐ PILOT BRIEFING	☐ VNR	TIME STARTED	SPECIALIST INITIALS
	☐ STOPOVER			

1. TYPE	2. AIRCRAFT IDENTIFICATION	3. AIRCRAFT TYPE / SPECIAL EQUIPMENT	4. TRUE AIRSPEED	5. DEPARTURE POINT	6. DEPARTURE TIME		7. CRUISING ALTITUDE
VFR	N60458	Cessna T182T/G	150	MYF	PROPOSED (Z)	ACTUAL (Z)	6,000
✓ IFR			KTS		15:30		
DVFR							

8. ROUTE OF FLIGHT

MZB V23 LAX V299 VTU V25 RZS DIRECT

9. DESTINATION (Name of airport and city)	10. EST. TIME ENROUTE		11. REMARKS
	HOURS	MINUTES	
IZA	1	20	

12. FUEL ON BOARD		13. ALTERNATE AIRPORT(S)	14. PILOT'S NAME, ADDRESS & TELEPHONE NUMBER & AIRCRAFT HOME BASE	15. NUMBER ABOARD
HOURS	MINUTES		Profile on file	
5	30		17. DESTINATION CONTACT/TELEPHONE (OPTIONAL)	4
			Profile on file	

16. COLOR OF AIRCRAFT	CIVIL AIRCRAFT PILOTS. FAR Part 91 requires you file an IFR flight plan to operate under instrument flight rules in controlled airspace. Failure to file could result in a civil penalty not to exceed $1,000 for each violation (Section 901 of the Federal Aviation Act of 1958, as amended). Filing of a VFR flight plan is recommended as a good operating practice. See also Part 99 for requirements concerning DVFR flight plans.
Red on White	

FAA Form 7233-1 (8-82)
Electronic Version (Adobe)

CLOSE VFR FLIGHT PLAN WITH _____ FSS ON ARRIVAL

It appears to you that your pilot has elected not to file a flight plan with the FAA.

Although a pilot is not required to file a flight plan to fly in clear weather, doing so will guarantee that should your pilot be forced to land off-airport, somewhere in the wilderness, search-and-rescue personnel will be dispatched to look for you and the other passengers on the airplane. The pilot not filing a flight plan should make you think yellow flag.

Aerobatic Maneuvers

Your pilot suggests that he or she demonstrate some aerobatic maneuvers while you and the other passengers are in the airplane.

There are certain aerobatic maneuvers that are legal, exciting, and, for many, fun to experience. However, mixing such maneuvers with the structured discipline required to successfully use the airplane as a transportation tool may distract the pilot and result in much more thrill than you bargained for. So the plan to do such maneuvers should make you think yellow flag.

31

Nonpilot Passengers

While you and the other passengers are boarding the airplane, you notice that the pilot has put a nonpilot passenger in the right-front seat, which is equipped with a full set of flight controls that are identical to those provided to the pilot on the left-hand side.

Such an arrangement should, under most circumstances, work out fine. Nevertheless, having two pilots up front, each with a full set of flight controls, is less risky than having just one pilot up front. However, it would be wise for the pilot to spend a few extra minutes explaining to the right-front nonpilot passenger that he or she should not touch the control wheel (or the "side-stick" control) or the peddles on the floor during the flight or while the airplane is moving on the ground. Moreover, it would be a good idea to explain that grabbing and moving the control wheel could compromise the pilot's ability to control the airplane. Seating nonpilot passengers within reach of the flight controls without a customized briefing should make you think yellow flag.

Trust Your Gut

32

Your pilot appears to be a bit of a braggart, and seems a bit strange, overly boastful, tends to exaggerate, play loose with the truth, and gives you the feeling the he or she is a bit of an adrenaline junkie.

In this situation, you may want to just trust your intuition. If you have a strong feeling of foreboding, your feelings very well may be correct.

If your pilot is a stranger to you, or someone you have only recently met, or even if he or she is someone you have known for a long time, and even if you have not observed any red flag or yellow flag behaviors, you may have to rely on your intuition. For example, does your pilot appear to be a braggadocio, exaggerate, play loose with the truth, or appear to be an adrenaline junkie. Here, your best option may be to listen to, and trust, your gut. In which case, you may have to decline being a passenger and indicate that you are not feeling well. This is especially important if you have observed yellow flag behaviors such as being rushed, improper fueling, or poor weather planning.

33

Learning to Fly

In order to have an enhanced feeling of control while flying in private airplanes as a passenger, you might consider learning how to fly yourself.

You can investigate this option by visiting flying schools or flying clubs at your local airport. Or you could contact the Aircraft Owners and Pilots Association (www.AOPA.org), where you will find a vast amount of information about learning to fly your own (or rented) airplane. If you wish, you could arrange to take one or two flight lessons, or you could continue with the entire series of lessons needed to be awarded the private pilot certificate. Either way, it is likely that you will feel much more confident and less anxious about being a passenger in a private airplane.

If you tend to be a front-seat passenger, the AOPA can point you toward "pinch hitter" courses that will teach you how to use the aircraft radio to declare an emergency and get help, fly the airplane to a nearby airport, and land the airplane should your pilot become incapacitated. Such courses usually consist of four hours of lecture presentations and four hours of flight instruction in the airplane. Some pinch hitter courses are offered online.